How to Raise Smart and Intelligent Children

7 Secrets for Raising a Successful and Thriving Child With Extraordinary Intelligence

Frank Dixon

Before we begin, I have something special waiting for you. An action-packed 1 page printout with a few quick & easy tips taken from this book that you can start using today to become a better parent right now!

It's my gift to you, free of cost. Think of it as my way of saying thank you to you for purchasing this book.

Claim your download of Profoundly Positive Parenting with Frank Dixon by scanning the QR code below and join my mailing list.

Sign up below to grab your free copy, print it out and hang it on the fridge!

Sign Up By Scanning The QR Code With Your Phone's Camera To Be Redirected To A Page To Enter Your Email And Receive INSTANT Access To Your Download

Before we jump in, I'd like to express my gratitude. I know this mustn't be the first book you came across and yet you still decided to give it a read. There are numerous courses and guides you could have picked instead that promise to make you an ideal and well-rounded parent while raising your children to be the best they can be.

But for some reason, mine stood out from the rest and this makes me the happiest person on the planet right now. If you stick with it, I promise this will be a worthwhile read.

In the pages that follow, you're going to learn the best parenting skills so that your child can grow to become the best version of themselves and in doing so experience a meaningful understanding of what it means to be an effective parent.

Notable Quotes About Parenting

"Children Must Be Taught How To Think, Not What To Think."

– Margaret Mead

"It's easier to build strong children than to fix broken men [or women]."

- Frederick Douglass

"Truly great friends are hard to find, difficult to leave, and impossible to forget."

– George Randolf

"Nothing in life is to be feared, it is only to be understood. Now is the time to understand more, so that we may fear less."

– Scientist Marie Curie

Table of Contents

Introduction

Every parent dreams of a bright, happy, and successful future for their child. They want to see them ace their grades, get high-paying jobs, and have meaningful and loving relationships. They want intelligent kids who can vouch for themselves, have the resilience to bounce back, express and attend to their emotional needs, and have excellent social and life skills. It doesn't matter what path they choose as long as they are happy and satisfied with their lives.

For decades, intelligence and smartness were thought to be innate traits. Some children had it, and some didn't. People believed that you had to be born with it. It wasn't a skill that you can learn, hone, and excel in. But with recent findings and research, it is becoming clearer that intelligence is no longer white and black. Intelligence is no longer measured by how much one scores academically. Emotional and cognitive intelligence is just as important. You don't have to be a computer genius or a surgeon to be intelligent. You can be a musician, a marketing executive, or a shop owner and be as intelligent as a doctor or computer geek.

Today, an individual that possesses flexibility in their thinking, has a growth mindset, thinks before speaking, and regulates their emotions well is intelligent. If we look at all these characteristics, we realize that to be intelligent; one doesn't have to read 100 books a year. You may finish one and be as smart as others in your class, workplace, or family.

Since it is no longer considered a virtue that one possesses, it means we can improve and harness it. A parent(s) can play a key role in this. A curious, disciplined, and well-developed mind is an advantage in all human activities, from academics to relationships.

How parents interact with their kids plays a significant role in how smart they become. Your role is to prepare them to become independent, emotionally intelligent, and confident. Only then can they achieve what they set their heart to.

A child's brain isn't a miniature version of an adult's brain, as supposed earlier. It is a brain under construction that connects itself to the world. All your child sees, hears, touches, and smells becomes a part of who they are. New connections are formed every minute as a child learns to link two instructions with each other. Therefore, parents can create a world that is rich with connecting rules and choices.

When it comes to nature vs. nurture, intelligence seems to have a 50/50 split. Meaning, some of it is based on genetic predisposition, whereas the remaining half is based on the learning and influences from the external environment. Strong parental influence can impact not just how intelligent our children believe themselves to be, but also how smart they really are.

This doesn't mean that you inundate your child with foreign language courses, tennis tutorship, or math drills before they have even learned to walk themselves. It means that you must focus on habits and behaviors that foster growth and an intellectual mindset. You must stop praising their innate acumen and start cultivating skills and habits that help them increase their intelligence and become smarter than others.

This is the goal of this book—to help parents promote habits and practices that improve intelligence and raise children with extraordinary intelligence. The book talks about seven secrets to help parents reach that goal and see their child grow into a successful and intellectual adult.

Chapter 1:

Measuring Intelligence

In 1904, members of the Paris school board approached a psychologist with a unique and odd request. It was the time when psychology was evolving as an independent field. The request was to create an objective method to rate a child's smartness so that children with poor intelligence could be offered intervention and special education. During that time, children were either seen as gifted or intellectually disabled. However, there was no in-between scale to measure how smart or dumb they were. Alfred Binet, who was already working on similar topics agreed and enlisted his colleague, Theodore Simon, to join as well (Cherry, 2020).

While designing the test, both psychologists knew that they had to use items and questions every child could answer without study or training. The idea was to create a task that could measure the ability of children to handle intellectual tasks—not the kind of knowledge they acquired in school.

Binet and Simon decided to use items of two different types. One was so unusual that no children would have any prior experience of using them, and second was so familiar that almost all children would have been exposed to them in the past. In the test, children were expected to perform the following tasks:

- Follow simple commands or copy gestures
- Name objects in the pictures attached
- Repeat a sentence of 15 words
- Differentiate between two common objects
- Finish off incomplete sentences left by the examiner

The first version took a year to develop, and Binet and Simon published it in 1905. It contained 30 items. It was well-received by the public and proved to be quite effective. Using the test, schools were ready to identify students with learning disabilities requiring special education (Cherry, 2020).

Encouraged by its success, the psychologists broadened the scope of their test to measure a child's intelligence and the variations in it. They published a revised version of their test in 1908 in which they grouped items by age. Each level then had six items designed for children from 3 to 13 years. All items were placed at a particular age level after 75% of the children in that age group could guess them correctly.

Many countries revised and used Binet's tests. In the U.S., Lewis Terman, a Stanford University psychologist, developed the Stanford-Binet test. The test was soon adopted in different settings across the country. Over the years, psychologists continued to revise the tests. One of the key features that made the Stanford-Binet test stand out from the earlier tests was that it yielded a single score every time. That single score reflected a person's intelligence levels (IQ).

Initially, the letters IQ stood for intelligence quotient. The quotient represented the scores of the result. To obtain an IQ score, the formula they applied involved dividing the student's mental age by their chronological age. They then multiplied the number by 100. Mental age was assessed by the number of items a student passed correctly on the test. Every correct answer yielded the students with two months' credit of mental age.

In case the mental and chronological ages came to be equal, it meant that the person had an IQ of 100. This came down to be an average score. Test takers that obtained a score above 100 were regarded as more intelligent than typical students in the same age bracket. Test takers that obtained a score lower than 100 were considered less intelligent than their peers.

However, you might have spotted a problem with this score. What was supposed to happen when mental growth levels halted, and the individual's chronological age continued to grow? As expected, intelligence quotients started to decline after early teen years. This led examiners to think of another formula and definition for IQ.

To counter this problem, psychologist David Wechsler devised a set of tests that included performance, nonverbal, and verbal items. They were designed for both adults and children. The tests yielded separate scores for two components of intelligence. Since he developed those tests during a time when the multifaceted nature of intelligence wasn't fully understood, we can't say for certain whether his previous subtests measured different aspects of intelligence or not.

However, after some time, the Wechsler tests became the most popular tests to rate one's intelligence and are currently used in different areas of aptitude to test how smart one is.

How Do We Measure Intelligence?

We take intelligence tests to know how well someone can think. We can identify areas of expertise where someone thinks well and also areas in which they lack. This way, we can better understand the corresponding strengths and weaknesses. The pattern of someone's strengths and weaknesses in thinking allows examiners and teachers to decide if someone is a disabled learner or not. It also encourages parents to begin intervention programs directed to treat a specific learning disorder. However, the way we measure a student's thinking is not confounded by the things they know. Therefore, as an examiner or teacher, one must interpret the test scores by asking the students to get the answer right and how they may have to think.

As discussed earlier, the Wechsler Adult Intelligence Scale is the most commonly used intelligence test for adults today. There are different versions of the test, referred to as WAIS and WAIS-IV. The WAIS-IV was standardized on 2,200 people within the age bracket of 16 to 90. The test consists of 15 tasks, each designed to measure intelligence. The 15 tasks assigned include working memory, spatial ability, math ability, and general knowledge about the world.

The test yields scores on four domains: working memory, verbal, perpetual, and processing speed. The WAIS-IV reliability is 0.95, which exhibits substantial construct validity. The Wechsler Scale has also been adopted by many school districts for preschool children called the Wechsler Primary and Preschool Scale of Intelligence (WPPSI-III). For adolescents and older children, it comes in the form of the Wechsler Intelligence Scale for Children (WISC-IV).

The intelligence tests are mostly used to interpret one's aptitude and are designed to measure a student's ability to perform any given task. These tests are used by many schools for enrollment and examination purposes. You may be familiar with the Scholastic Assessment Test (SAT) or the American College Test (ACT) that students are required to take for grade admissions. Post-graduate programs in the U.S. also require the Graduate Record Examination (GRE), Law School Admission Test (LSAT), Graduate Management

Admission Test (GMAT), and Medical College Admissions Test (MCAT).

These tests are efficient by helping recruiters hire the right pool of candidates. Success in these tests predicts success in academics and professional careers.

Having learned about how we measure intelligence and what different tests and scales are used to rate one's IQ, parents can prepare children to practice for tests and ace them. Engaging in materials that compels one to think differently and problem-solve better can raise intelligence and smartness. However, to do that, you must know where your child stands in terms of their intelligence.

This is the first secret to raising intelligent children—identifying how smart they already are and what more needs to be done. In the different theories, we shall decode a child's core interest and passions and take it forward from there. Assessing how smart your child is the key to unlocking the amount of work you need to do. So let's get on with the seven secrets to raising an intelligent child.

Chapter 2:

What Kind of Smart Is My Kid?

At many points in history, different researchers have interpreted the meaning of intelligence differently. Some believe it to be academic knowledge whereas other schools of thought view it as the perfect balance between social and life skills. Some regard it as an effort to problem solve and recognize them earlier than others. While these definitions may vary considerably, the most recent conceptualization suggests that intelligence is one's ability to:

- Learn from experience: This involves the acquisition, retention, and use of new information

- Recognition and assessment of problems: This involves the utilization of learned knowledge for the identification of possible problems in the surrounding that need addressing.

- Solution of problems: This involves coming up with viable solutions for the identified problems and putting your best ideas to work.

Intelligence involves different mental abilities like reasoning, logic, problem-solving, and planning. While the subject is of most interest to scientists, psychologists, and researchers alike, it is still believed to be one of the most controversial ones as well. Psychologists may disagree about the definitions and reasons for intelligence, but the research we have on intelligence plays a significant role in different settings. For example, by measuring intelligence, important decisions about school funding can be made; new educational programs and interventions may be discussed; screening of job applicants may take place; and children requiring additional help with their studies may receive the said help.

Since it is a topic with great controversy, there are different theories about intelligence that provide valuable insights on how one assesses intelligence in children and adults. In this chapter, we shall discuss these theories in depth—particularly the one by Howard Gardner—as they help us determine how smart and intelligent our children are and how we can nurture this quality. This is the first and most important secret to raising intelligent children.

Theories of Intelligence

Here are some of the most talked-about theories that emerged during the last 100 years.

General Intelligence

In 1904, British psychologist Charles Spearman described a concept that he called the "g factor" or general intelligence. After using the technique called factor analysis (Spearman, 1904), he examined some mental aptitude tests. He concluded that the scores he gained from these tests were similar to the ones on the Wechsler Scale. According to him, students that performed well on one cognitive test also performed well on other tests. Similarly, those that performed badly on one test tended to score badly on other tests as well. Therefore, he concluded that intelligence is a general cognitive ability that we can measure and express numerically (Spearman, 1904).

Primary Mental Abilities

In 1973, psychologist Louis, L. Thurstone, put forth a differing theory of intelligence, viewing it as a combination of seven primary mental abilities (Thurstone, 1973). These include:

1. Associative memory: the aptitude to memorize and recall
2. Perceptual speed: the aptitude to see similarities/differences among objects
3. Numerical ability: the aptitude to solve math problems
4. Reasoning: Aptitude to look for rules
5. Verbal comprehension: the aptitude to understand and define words
6. Spatial visualization: the aptitude to visualize connections and relationships
7. Word fluency: the aptitude to produce and pronounce words rapidly

Theory of Multiple Intelligences

A Harvard professor and psychologist, Howard Gardner, presented his theory of multiple intelligences in his book, *Frames of the Mind: The Theory of Multiple Intelligences*. He explains that individuals don't have a set of intellectual abilities but rather many kinds of intelligence. For instance, some may be good with musical notes but terrible with numbers. Some may look at things logically while others interpret life interpersonally. He argues that traditional psychometric views of intelligence and how it is measured are too narrow. They can't possibly capture one's abilities and talents in a single score. He thinks that there are more than two or three factors to judge someone's cognitive development (Gardner, 1983). He presents nine different types of intelligence in his theory of multiple intelligences, as will be shown below.

Logical-Mathematical Intelligence

Logical-mathematical intelligence is a unique form of intelligence in which a person knows the answers to a problem long before they verbalize it. Children identified as logical-mathematical intelligent are good at solving puzzles, mysteries, brainteasers, and logic-based exercises. They can count or do calculations in their mind, solve computer problems, and attain top scores in strategy-building games. This type of intelligence is most similar to general intelligence we studied earlier. Children with this type of intelligence recognize patterns easier and view problems from a rational point of view. They can reason well and negotiate their way out of a deal. Their excellent communication skills can even get them out of trouble.

Ideal careers for children with logical-mathematical intelligence include:

- Economist
- Computer Programmer
- Mathematician

- Scientist
- Accountant
- Engineer

Naturalistic Intelligence

Children with this type of intelligence are more drawn toward environmental issues, animals, and plants. They are more involved in outdoor activities like hiking, camping, caring for animals, recycling, and learning/caring for nature. They have an innate ability to connect with pets and wild animals alike; they feel at peace when out in nature. They are sensitive to the natural world. They feel like it is their responsibility to nurture and explore the world. They are the first ones to raise their voice against the effects of climate change.

Ideal career choices for naturalistic intelligent children include:

- Farmer
- Geologist
- Botanist
- Conservationist
- Biologist
- Florist

Linguistic Intelligence

Children with linguistic intelligence are skilled in activities like reading, storytelling, talking, telling jokes, writing poems, playing word games, and learning languages. This is the most common type of intelligence. It involves one's ability to think in words and use words to help others understand them. These people are expressive and can give their emotions and feelings a voice.

Ideal careers for those with linguistic intelligence include:

- Novelist
- Poet
- Editor
- Journalist
- Lawyer
- English Professor

Spatial Intelligence

Children with spatial intelligence can consider things in three dimensions. They are good at solving spatial challenges like drawing, reading maps, painting, looking at pictures, playing construction games, solving mazes, etc. Children with high spatial intelligence are creative in general. They possess a vivid imagination, excellent spatial reasoning, and a high artistic ability. They can often be referred to as "picture smart."

Ideal career choices for such creative individuals include:

- Architect
- Pilot
- Fashion Designer
- Surgeon
- Artist

Musical Intelligence

Children with musical intelligence have a natural tendency to learn different sounds, sing, play musical instruments, compose new tunes, enjoy listening to music, and follow various rhythms. They may be quick to notice any off-key notes that others miss out on.

Memorizing tunes and lyrics come naturally to them. They are drawn toward quality music. People with musical intelligence are sensitive to sounds and can pick up noises that many don't. They can differentiate between different pitches and tones and reveal a keen interest in playing music.

That being said, it shouldn't come as a surprise that these children can make promising careers in:

- Singing
- Composing music
- Writing poems
- DJing
- Teaching Music
- Songwriting

Interpersonal Intelligence

Interpersonal intelligence is common in children that are good at communication. They can talk, collaborate, help others, mediate conflicts, and meet new people effortlessly. They have this natural ability to make others feel comfortable around them. They are approachable and social. These people can read both verbal and nonverbal cues and decipher one's mood and temperament. They are also empathetic. This type of intelligence is most commonly associated with life coaches, leaders, social workers, and psychologists.

Ideal careers for people with interpersonal intelligence include:

- Team Manager
- Politician

- Negotiator
- Salesperson
- Publicist
- Psychologist

Intrapersonal Intelligence

Children with intrapersonal intelligence know themselves best. They appreciate independence. They like to set goals and focus on achieving them. They have a knack for understanding the feelings of others as well as knowing their strengths and weaknesses very well. Intrapersonal intelligence allows children to understand themselves and the human condition as a whole. We can call them self-smart people. They may appear social and approachable, but they are mostly shy. People with intrapersonal intelligence make for good spiritual leaders, writers, philosophers, and psychologists.

Potential career choices for those with intrapersonal intelligence include

- Therapist
- Entrepreneur
- Counselor
- Psychologist

- Theorist
- Philosopher

Bodily-Kinesthetic Intelligence

Children with this type of intelligence use their whole bodies to express their ideas and emotions. They use their hands and arms extensively to express feelings. They have an exceptional sense of timing and great overall body coordination. Their gross and fine motor skills are also commendable. They use their body expressively and therefore are usually great at taking roles in dancing, medicine, and sports. They can act well, imitate gestures, play sports, and move freely.

Excellent career choices for those with bodily-kinesthetic Intelligence include:

- Dancing
- Physical therapist
- Mechanic
- Athlete
- Actor
- Builder

Triarchic Theory of Intelligence

The triarchic theory of intelligence was proposed by Robert Sternberg in 1988. He viewed intelligence as a combination of three parts: analytical, creative, and practical. His theory is based on a broader definition of intelligence than other psychologists. He defines it in the terms of one's ability to achieve success based on their stance in a sociocultural context. He believes that the ability to achieve success depends on the aptitude to capitalize on one's strengths and compensate for one's weaknesses. According to the theory, we can attain success through a balance of creative, analytical, and practical abilities. This balance is needed to adapt, shape, and select environments, as we will see below ("Intelligence and Creativity," n.d.).

1. Analytical intelligence: Analytical intelligence is aligned closely with academic computation and problem-solving. Analytical intelligence is demonstrated by the ability to evaluate, analyze, compare, judge, and contrast. For example, when you read a novel, you compare the motives of the central characters. Based on that knowledge, you analyze the historical context of the story.

2. Practical intelligence: Practical intelligence is a lot like having "street smarts." When someone says they are practical, it means that they can

find solutions in their everyday life by applying the knowledge they gained through experiences.

3. Creative intelligence: Creative intelligence involves inventing and imagining a solution to a problem or circumstance. Creativity means finding novel solutions to a new problem or producing a work of art that is out of the box. Think of it as someone that comes up with a solution to stay warm during a camping trip when you forget to pack extra blankets.

Having discussed these various theories around intelligence, we can assess what kind of "smart" our children are. For example, they may be good at playing instruments or express themselves through artistic endeavors like dancing or acting. They may be good with words or numbers. They may have an innate love for nature or prefer to be shy in social circles. Whatever quality makes them stand out is the type of intelligence they possess.

As a parent, it is our job to nurture that and increase intelligence. How can we do that? The following chapters reveal the remaining six secrets to helping children thrive with confidence and knowledge. With the help of some valuable research, activities, and games, we can raise children who are mentally competent, happy, and incredibly smart.

Chapter 3:

Social Skills Learning

Learning social skills prepares children for life—not just school or career. Good social skills allow children to communicate, express themselves, and interact with others positively and confidently. They can easily read between the lines and uncover one's gestures, body language, and facial expressions. Since we are social animals, our dependence on one another is a given. We were created to live in harmony, prosper as a community, and be a source of help for others.

Throughout the years, we have learned different ways of communication and expression. We have invented tools and scales to measure our social compatibility with others. We have fashioned predictability meters that rate one's social skills and determine what careers and fields they are most likely to succeed in.

Since the goal is to raise intelligent and sensible children, social skills building is the first and most important secret. Social skills are essential for improving both personal and professional relationships. Strong interpersonal skills make it easier for children to accomplish career goals, perform at their best during the recruitment process, and contribute to their company's achievements. With good social competence, they can expand their professional network and land better-earning opportunities.

Besides academic success, high levels of social competence also predict better academic outlines in math and reading among children in disadvantaged communities (Elias & Haynes, 2008).

Improved social skills also increase the likelihood of success in a professional setting. Those with good social skills do well in their jobs, despite having low support from their administration. Social skills help employees that need cooperation and resources to do well (Hochwarter et al., 2006).

But professional life isn't the only predictor of success in life. How well we do in our relationships also reveals our levels of happiness and satisfaction in life. Studies suggest that children with strong social competence blend well with their peers and are likely to have more meaningful friendships. They also find meeting new people and befriending them easier. This was concluded in a study published in the *International Encyclopedia of the Social & Behavioral Sciences* (Borner et al., 2015).

Important Social Skills to Teach Your Children

Since social skills increase a child's chances of forming deeper relationships, increasing wellness, and feeling confident and worthy, we must know what specific skills will help them increase their intelligence as well. As being intelligent requires problem-solving skills, a growth mindset, and flexibility in thinking, below are 10 important aspects of social skills that we must nurture in children.

Effective Communication

Effective communication is the art of effectively communicating with others. Strong communication skills allow children to express their thoughts and ideas more clearly. They can speak their mind when they can find the right words, tone, and pitch. Effective communicators often have a large social circle and make for great leaders, too.

Following Instructions

An important aspect of social skills is following instructions. Children that struggle with directions end up with a variety of consequences. For example, they may have to redo their homework, as they didn't listen to the instructions correctly the first time. They may also have trouble with chores and tasks that require attempting multiple things.

Respecting Personal Space

You must teach children to respect one's personal space. Sometimes, they may not get the idea that their closeness makes others feel uncomfortable. Some children may even crawl in the laps of acquaintances and not realize how it makes them feel. Similarly, they may try to act ill-mannered in public places and try to get into another person's business. This isn't seen as good parenting, so teach them to maintain a two-feet distance when speaking to someone and to keep their hands to themselves.

Cooperation

Cooperation is similar to sharing, as it requires children to work together to achieve a common goal. When we say we want to teach collaboration, we are actually saying that we want to raise respectful children when others make requests. It involves assisting others and active participation. Good cooperation skills are imperative for the well-being and survival within a community as well. Raising a breed of children that respect and accept each other without judgment and prejudice is more important than ever.

Listening

The definition of listening may be as simple as staying quiet while others speak. However, there is more to it than meets the eye. Listening involves the absorption of information. Listening is an important aspect of healthy communication. So much depends on your child's ability to listen and absorb. From taking notes to doing homework, from doing chores to following instructions, there is a lot that relies on how competent the child is at listening.

Good Manners

Parents must also teach children good etiquette and manners. Gestures as simple as saying thank-you, bowing in gratitude, and knocking on a door before entering count as good manners. Good manners allow children to get respect and attention for all the right reasons. Well-disciplined and well-mannered children and adults are admirable by all.

Sharing

The act of sharing and collaborating is something that organizations seek in ideal employees. Employers want people who can work as team members and provide valuable input. Teaching children to share with others also helps them make and keep friends. According to one study, children as little as two exhibit a desire to share with others, given the resources are abundant (Spearman, 1904). If this is true, all we need to offer is an abundance of resources and the skill will itself manifest.

Conflict Resolution

Dissatisfaction and disagreement can arise in the simplest of situations. Conflict resolution is an ability that allows children to get to the source of it and come up with a workable solution. Conflict resolution skills are important not only in personal life but also professionally. Children with strong conflict resolution skills can prevent getting into verbal and physical fights with their peers. In case a fight breaks out, they can resolve it calmly and logically.

Empathy

Empathy is the art of listening to someone without judgment. It involves understanding and identifying with the feelings of others. It involves noticing their facial expressions, gestures, and body language. It requires that you make others feel supported and taken care of. Teaching children to be empathic from an early age can make them kind and compassionate. It can help build rapport and make them stronger.

Relationship Management

Relationship management involves maintaining healthy relationships with everyone. It is crucial for building key relationships. To teach relationship management to kids, you must act as a role model and be kind and respectful to everyone around you. You must voice your concerns respectably and work on improving your companionship by offering help, appreciation, and affection. You must address and resolve any conflicts that arise and take into consideration the well-being of others.

Activities and Games That Promote Social Skills Building

To make social skills learning fun and engaging for young ones, in this section, we look at some interesting and simple activities that will help children improve their communication, emotional regulation, and self-discipline.

Staring Contest

Most children with a learning disability like autism or Asperger's syndrome have trouble maintaining eye contact with others. They can't have normal conversations with their peers and teachers. This affects their self-confidence and self-worth. Other children are simply shy and don't enjoy being the center of attention.

A staring contest helps children learn about maintaining eye contact. They can learn to make as well as keep eye contact during conversations. It can also help students who get distracted easily and want to build focus.

Emotion Charades

Emotion charades are classic charades with a twist. Instead of naming movies, you name different emotions based on how they are enacted. All you need are a few strips of paper with different emotions named. You and your child can take turns by picking a slip and acting out the emotion. Allowing your child to enact an emotion will help them understand how to read the faces and body language of others. They can predict someone's mood and temperament better if they focus on their facial expressions a little. It can also help children regulate their emotions and give their feelings a name.

Play Pretend

Finally, to teach social skills, you must allow children to engage in pretend play. Give them ample opportunities and scenarios where they get to be someone or something. For instance, they may act like they are in a hospital and play the role of a doctor. They can look after patients, provide medicine, and assist where necessary. Similarly, they can pretend to be a teacher and teach hypothetical students in a classroom. Playing different roles and being in different scenarios will not only expand their knowledge about that field but also how they are expected to act. Each unique situation will help them develop social skills like commutation, empathy, coordination, collaboration, etc.

Improvisational Stories

Children love storybooks. They may like different genres, but their love for new stories is common. Some are natural storytellers. They love making up stories all the time. This is something that, as parents, we must foster. Storytelling, especially improvising on existing ones, is a great skill. Encourage children to place their favorite story characters into different challenging situations and ask them to find ways to overcome them. For instance, if a child has a fear of public speaking, you can ask them how their favorite character would present something in front of the whole class. With improvisational stories, you can mentally prepare them for tasks that they find difficult. You can also add rewards for coming up with the best story. Collaborating and allowing young children to create creative narratives without much thinking is another way to teach about different social skills.

Playing With Characters

For younger children, you can help them with the narrative using their stuffed toys and action figures as protagonists. You can use them to interact with your child and discuss important issues. For instance, during play, you can say things like, "I think Mr. Bugs Bunny is afraid of meeting new people. What can we do to help him?" Letting the child think and come up with strategies to counter such social situations can help them devise appropriate action plans. If your child is worried about performing on stage in front of an audience, you can help them by staging a show with their favorite toys and giving each toy a small skit to perform. You can also get other family members involved where you all take one or two toys and pretend to play with them.

Using toys, you can also talk about feelings and emotions and teach your child suitable behaviors to address, label, and cope with them.

Chapter 4:

Read With Your Folks

According to one study involving identical twins, scientists aimed at gathering data that would help them understand the role of reading and early literacy skills in children and its effects on test scores and intelligence in children. After comparing the test scores of the pairs that ranged from 7 to 16, scientists found that the differences in reading during early childhood years affect later differences in intelligence (Ritchie et al., 2014). One of the children that read performed better in both verbal and nonverbal (reasoning) tests than the child that didn't read. Visible differences were seen between the children that read and those that didn't. These differences were present in children as young as seven, which suggests that early reading skills affect one's intellectual development.

But do we need to seek confirmation from studies to tell us that reading makes us smarter? Reading is the key to unlocking the gate of immeasurable knowledge. For teachers, it is easy to spot children with a higher aptitude and better reading skills during elementary school years. Children with a broader vocabulary—who can read without needing to be guided, pronounce words correctly, and have a love for reading in general—appear to be more intelligent than those who don't read. The greater a child's reading skills, the more they know and can learn. Over the years, avid readers can increase their intellectual stamina and know more about the world than their peers who don't read.

One obvious benefit of reading is an increased vocabulary. Research shows that an increased vocabulary leads to higher test scores in general intelligence (Suk, 2017). Good reading skills also improve one's writing skills. It also allows us to visualize new worlds, explore new cultures, and meet people we have never met before. It boosts creativity and imagination. Evidence suggests that early reading skills also mean higher intelligence in the future (Jerrim et al., 2020).

In another paper, researchers studied the effects of reading on a group of adults that began reading at an early age, those who were illiterate, and those who learned to read later in life. Results revealed that readers had a more developed visual processing center in the brain called the occipital lobe (Szwed et al., 2011). This means that readers can process any visual information effectively, promising enhanced creativity skills. Adults with a highly developed occipital lobe can make a decision confidently. The same study also looked at the parietal lobes responsible for processing and interpreting reading and writing comprehension. The parietal lobes were strengthened in readers as expected.

Another study used functional magnetic resonance imaging (fMRI) imaging to study the brains of avid readers as opposed to the occasional reader or an individual that never reads. Researchers concluded that reading helps the brain process information both verbally and visually (Buchweitz et al., 2009). People who don't read or seldom read encounter problems when trying to form a connection between verbal and visual information when presented at the same time.

Aside from the occipital lobe, the study found that parietal lobes were strengthened. While the occipital lobe is responsible for visual processing, the parietal lobes play a crucial role in reading comprehension and writing as well.

Books and Brain: How Does Reading Improve Intelligence?

Although studies and research help with acknowledging the importance of reading with and to children from an early age, we still need more knowledge on how reading affects intelligence. Unfortunately, there is no concise evidence that claims to do so; myriad studies suggest that reading doesn't make one intelligent or smart, but it changes the way the brain thinks, focuses, and processes information. The science behind intelligence and reading reveals that regular reading affects intelligence in three ways.

Crystallized Intelligence

At the baseline, reading helps children build crystallized intelligence. Crystallized intelligence is factual knowledge that someone knows. It involves knowing all the figures and data. People with higher crystallized intelligence are book smart. Their mind is an encyclopedia. More reading adds to their bank of information (Kyllonen & Christal, 1990).

Fluid Intelligence

Fluid intelligence, as the name suggests, is more abstract knowledge. Fluid intelligence involves problem-solving skills; detecting patterns and sequences; and gaining an overall understanding of crystallized intelligence. There is a reciprocal relationship between reading and intelligence (Cattell, 1963). Reading builds focus and attention. It allows the brain to detect more patterns and connections. Increased reading activity helps the brain absorb more abstract knowledge.

Emotional Intelligence

Emotional intelligence can be defined as the ability to make associations. Reading fiction has been linked with improving one's theory of mind (Kidd & Castano, 2013). Theory of mind can be described as the measurement of an individual's ability to understand others and empathize with them. Individuals who are avid fiction readers are better at identifying someone else's emotions. They do so because similar psychological processes navigate fiction and real relationships.

In another study, researchers asked undergraduates to read the novel *Pompeii* by Robert Harris due to its dramatic and page-turning plot. Their brains were scanned to review the effects. The images suggested that the links between the brain's language center, left temporal cortex, and central sulcus (a region responsible for handling and managing physical feelings and movement) remained enhanced. Thus, one can say that reading makes the body and mind feel more in general (Kidd & Castano, 2013).

In short, while reading may not directly affect your child's intelligence per se, it does increase knowledge about things they don't know, help them make sense of difficult patterns, and increase empathy.

Activities That Nurture the Love for Reading

Reading helps children learn about the world in imaginative ways. It expands their horizons. Reading can introduce them to different people and cultures. Nurturing good reading habits in children, therefore, is an important task. However, there is always a question that boggles parents, especially those who are raising picky readers or children who don't show any interest in the activity. How can we attract them? How can we turn them into avid readers and increase their chances of becoming highly intelligent?

Many experts suggest reading to children as little as six months old. Some say to engage them with illustrative art and audiobooks. Others are staunch believers that children will develop a love for reading if they see their parents read.

But these tips still don't offer any practical ideas. Since all children love to play games and engage in interactive activities, this is the best form of learning for young children, as they don't feel like they are being forced to read.

Guess the Word

This is an interesting and knowledgeable game for many reasons. For starters, it encourages children to learn new words, their meaning, and their usage. Second, their love for reading and exploration increases. Here's how you play it.

You start by writing a complex word on a slip of paper. You can create 5 to 10 slips, each with a unique word. Next, you ask your child to bring a dictionary. Each of you gets to pick a slip and read the word. The other person has to guess what the word is. Each member gets to ask five questions. Some examples of questions you may ask include:

- Is it a place, thing, or animal?

- How many vowels are there in the word?
- If it's a thing, it is in the house?
- What is its use?

Each of these questions leaves the child to do some thinking.

I Spy With Words

We are all familiar with this game, as we have played it countless times on drives and picnics with our friends and family. Have you ever thought that you can play it with your child at home?

Here's how. You are going to need a few interesting objects and a good vocabulary. Put together various objects you can find at home and ask your child to guess something surrounding those items. For example, if the item you picked is cereal, you say something like; "I spy something that we can eat in the morning that starts with C." You have to let your child decode the hint and get it right. As they grow older, you can make the game a tad bit harder and encourage the usage of new words to add to their vocabulary.

Young Scrabble

Scrabble is an all-time classic. It is loved by children and adults alike. It is an exciting and interactive game ideal to play with your child during their free time. The idea is simple, but you can add your twist to it. Instead of giving them just seven letters, give your child as many as possible, provided there is an abundance of vowels. Next, ask your child to come up with as many words as they can using the letters they have. You can even print out a list of three, four, and five-letter words. They get points for as many letters as they make.

Label Common Objects

To increase your child's literacy and reading skills, start early. Use index cards or sticky notes to label everyday items in your house. For example, label cupboard, fridge, lounge, laptop, dinner table, and other items. The goal is to improve reading and spelling. You can make it even more interesting by asking young children to place the index cards correctly on the items listed.

Chapter 5:

Regulate Screen Time

Television, social media, and video games have become every child's favorite pastime. They will spend hours and hours playing games and watching videos on social platforms. Tell them to open a book or engage in any physical activity, and they will make a ton of excuses why they don't have time for them.

As parents, our goal should be to provide our children with more stimulating activities instead. Besides, there is evidence which concludes that watching television stunts or limits a child's intellectual growth. According to one study by researchers in the U.K., screen time that exceeds three hours per day leads to cognitive decline in memory and language down the line (Fancourt & Steptoe, 2019).

Researchers looked at data from the *English Longitudinal Study of [Aging]* (ELSA). They looked at data from 3,662 adults above the age of 50. In the data, participants had recorded the amount of time they spent watching TV daily. During this time, their thinking and reasoning skills were also measured. The researchers studied the cognitive measures of memory and language over six years from 2014 to 2015. They found that seniors who had watched 3.5 hours of TV every day experienced a decline in their verbal memory. It was greater as compared to the data of those who watched TV for less than 3.5 hours per day. The study, of course, excluded independent variants like overall physical health, socioeconomic status, and depression (Fancourt & Steptoe, 2019).

In another study, neuroscientists in Japan looked at brain imaging of 290 children between the ages of 5 and 18 (Takeuchi et al., 2013). They sorted data according to the number of hours those children spent watching TV. Images revealed significant anatomical differences in multiple brain regions that correlated with the amount of screen time viewed. Researchers then reexamined the same children many years later and saw many of the anatomical changes happening in their brains. The more hours children spend watching TV, the greater the changes in the brain's structure.

The reason this information is pivotal is that the regions that were most affected in the brain were responsible for emotional response, vision, arousal, and aggression. There was an increase in gray matter in the hypothalamus septum, visual cortex, sensory-motor areas, and frontal lobe. An increase in the gray matter is responsible for lowering verbal IQ. Further tests confirmed how children that enjoyed more screen time had low verbal IQ. It further declined depending on the hours children spent watching TV. Some changes were also visible beneath the cerebral cortex in the brain's wiring network. These were observable in children of all genders—regardless of their age, socioeconomic status, and other such factors.

Changes in the hypothalamus are characteristics of increased aggressiveness, borderline personality disorder, and mood disorders in children. They may act more stressed out and suffer from lower verbal IQ.

Dangers of Watching Too Much TV

The drawbacks don't stop there, either. There are many other disadvantages of excessive screen time. Children who are continuously plugged in with some device like TV, a tablet, or game consoles also report other issues.

According to some studies, children that watch TV for more than four hours per day are more likely to be obese (Rosiek et al., 2015). This is because of the lack of physical activity that makes the muscles idle and inflexible. Sitting for long hours at a time also leads to fat accumulation around the neck, stomach, and thigh areas. Obese children are at a higher risk for diabetes, heart disease, and high blood pressure.

There is also a high risk of exposure to negative or violent behaviors. Playing games and watching shows based on violence or sexual content normalizes those behaviors in one's mind. At first, it may be confusing and frightening for them. However, regular exposure can make them view those as acceptable. It can also turn them aggressive.

Exposure to risky behaviors like alcohol addiction, smoking, or binge eating is also a drawback of unsupervised screen time. Advertising of unhealthy foods and drinks is also common, something parents must restrict their children from. The more they see these products being advertised as tasty, scrumptious, and desirable, the more they'll want them.

Thus, it is important to regulate screen time. As parents, we must be strict and vigilant about the time children spend watching TV or playing games. We must also keep tabs on the type of content they are exposed to. Make sure that they aren't wasting hours watching videos that don't add to their knowledge or make them attracted to violent and risky behaviors.

Invest in Activities That Stimulate the Brain

So, if children don't watch TV, what should they spend their time doing? This is one of the excuses parents hear from their children often. What should we do then?

What they should be doing is engaging in activities and games that stimulate their brain instead. They should be doing things that improve their intelligence—not lower it. The following games and activities have been listed as some of the most amazing, engaging, and fun games that improve a child's focus, attention, and intelligence.

Jigsaw Puzzles

Finishing puzzles such as sudoku and jigsaw puzzles are a great way to exercise the brain. According to one study, playing board games and piecing puzzles together lowers the risk of cognitive impairments in adults (Krell-Roesch et al., 2017).

Memory Card Games

Memory card games are another beneficial and rewarding pastime. Memory games require children to remember patterns and sequences. They sharpen the mind by keeping it alert and focused (Global Council on Brain Health, 2017). They are a lot like exercise but for the brain. The more attentive and focused one's brain is, the more flexible it becomes. More flexibility means more space for the mind to process and interpret new information and ideas. These games are designed to test a child's short-term memory and improve recall and recognition.

Crossword Puzzles

Like sudoku and other jigsaw puzzles, crosswords puzzles are another favorite of many children. They can help children learn new words and remember their spelling. They are another excellent way to stimulate the brain and much better than watching TV. According to one study, crossword puzzles may be the answer to delaying age-related memory decline in adults (Pillai et al., 2011). Many researchers believe that it can delay the onset of diseases like preclinical dementia and Alzheimer's in adults.

Chess

Chess is another great way to keep the mind busy and alert. According to one study, playing chess leads to improvements in memory, increases the brain's information processing speed, and enhances overall executive functioning. With children, they are known to develop this perspective-taking ability (Gao et al., 2019).

Learn a New Skill

Apart from playing games, learning a new skill also gives the brain something new to work on. Learning a new language or skill requires ample knowledge, practice, and patience—things usually associated with improved intelligence. In one study, researchers observed seniors involved in a variety of skills from quilting to digital photography. During that time, they also did some memory tests. Compared to adults in the experimental and control groups, those who were involved in some skill-building activity experienced improvements on memory tests over time (Park et al., 2013). These memory improvements were still noticeable after a year.

Use Nondominant Hand

According to neurobiologists, this one activity, although challenging, helps keep the brain alive. Lawrence C. Katz and Manning Rubin, in their book, *Keep Your Brain Alive: 83 Neurobic Exercises to Help Prevent Memory Loss and Increase Mental Fitness*, talk about how using your nondominant hand strengthens the mind. They insist on making children try using their nondominant hand from the start so that they can be in the practice of using it. This activity increases brain functioning, as the brain has to focus more on what's being done. Switching hands while eating or doing homework awakens the mind in an instant (Katz & Rubin, 1998).

Chapter 6:

Raise Them to Be Problem Solvers

Problem-solving is a process that involves finding answers or solutions for a current question or problem. The solution usually ends with a path that leads to success or the ultimate goal. Intelligence and problem-solving skills have long been connected. Nearly all definitions of intelligence include an element of problem-solving skills. Problem-solving skills in children are a predictor of how smart, vigilant, and devoted they are mentally.

According to one study, children that lack problem-solving skills are at an increased risk of developing mental health problems in children. They are more likely to experience symptoms of depression and suicide. Research also provides evidence that teaching young children problem-solving skills from an early age also makes them more resilient in the face of adversity and challenges (Becker-Weidman et al., 2010). They seem more prepared to deal with new and unforeseen circumstances.

As parents, we want to protect our children from all harm and danger. We want to keep them close to ourselves at all times and notice all their activities and engagement. However, this isn't possible, especially when they start school. There, they are on their own to fend for themselves. Teachers may or may not be available to supervise their activities at all times. Therefore, we must prepare them to handle problems they face themselves. This involves making new friends, collaborating on projects, and avoiding conflicts and fights with their peers.

Chances are, they are going to have a taste of all these at least once in their academic life. Therefore, they must have the skills to advocate for themselves and find solutions to problems they face. Children who lack basic problem-solving skills may land themselves in situations that are hard to get out of. For example, if they can't raise their voice against bullying, they may get bullied more. If they struggle to deal with conflicts among friends, they may not have friends at all.

Additionally, they may resort to behaviors that are inappropriate and violent. If a child doesn't know how to respond to someone cutting the line in front of them, they might resort to physical violence and start a fight. Alternatively, they may become scared and run away. Both of these solutions don't address the core problem and remain one.

Problem-solving skills teach children that they have choices. They make them put more pressure on their brains to find a solution that works for everybody. They teach children to think before reacting. Their calculated and well-thought response can keep their impulsiveness at bay.

How Problem-Solving Skills Help Kids

Problem-solving skills for children are important, as they improve their academic performance as well. They teach children discernment. They can feel well-equipped to distinguish between solvable and unsolvable problems. This will prevent the wastage of time, energy, and resources. They can invest their energies elsewhere and improve their other skills.

Sometimes, it takes a whole team to solve a problem. In school, it can translate into wanting to win a game against another team with a defining strategy. In exams, it can mean working together to go through all lectures and notes. It may require more than one person, as many students divide chapters and then study in a group by presenting all the key points discussed in the chapter. The point is, they might need to collaborate and work together. They might also have to take risks and seek help from others. This means that they will eventually need to ask themselves some determining questions such as:

- How can we make this challenge less intimidating?
- What solutions can be best applied to solve this?
- How can we work as a team and use our unique strengths to solve this?

Asking such questions and seeking their answers allow children to develop a deeper understanding of cause and effect. They can also improve their reflective and critical thinking skills.

Problem-solving skills have also been linked with improved self-confidence and grit. Finding solutions means making choices. It involves finding workable solutions that are efficient and effective. Not everything works out right the first time, so they can either surrender or work harder. Those who decide to not give up need better solutions and a fresh perspective to restart. They need to take more calculated risks to avoid failure.

When they try another time and succeed, they feel confident and proud of themselves. They feel capable of improving on existing solutions and growing further. This often leads to better time management skills and patience. It also allows children to assess their strengths and weaknesses and become more aware of how much courage they have within themselves.

For children, even the simplest of problems can appear challenging. This can cause stress and anxiety, damaging mental peace. However, if they know of healthy ways to prevent and cope with stress, they can become better problem solvers and emotional regulators. They can learn to handle everyday stresses and overcome them victoriously.

As parents, we must strengthen and nurture problem-solving skills in them so that they feel ready for anything life puts on their plate. They can avoid having a meltdown or tantrum when things don't go the way they expected them to go.

Problem-solving skills can help raise smart and independent children. They can be more confident in their abilities and accountable for their actions. They can become resilient and face difficulties head-on. When they have good problem-solving skills, they can view each problem as a unique problem, address it, and deal with it by evoking lateral thinking. Unlike children who are afraid of trying new things, children with problem-solving skills use their imagination, creativity, and confidence to steer clear of their problems without losing hope or their mind.

Activities That Nurture Investigative Skills in Children

Teaching children to problem solve has to start at home. We are their teachers and guide. We have to provide them with role model behavior. They should have ample opportunities to observe us deal with our problems. If they see you yelling on the phone because a shipment got delayed, crying because you forgot to save an important document on your laptop, or letting stress get to you by biting your nails and pacing in and out of the room, then they are going to follow suit. They will assume it to be the right way to deal with any upsets they encounter.

Therefore, the first step is to provide them with examples from your own life. Talk about your struggles, failures, and achievements. Emphasize on roadblocks that you experienced in your path and how you overcame them. Talk about the joy and sense of joy that followed after to make them view the habit as a positive and rewarding one.

Apart from that, below are some activities and games that will help you instill good problem-solving skills in your children from an early age.

Impromptu Solutions

Before starting, think of a few problems that your child may encounter and write them out on paper. Make sure the challenges are relatable to the situation or venue they are at. For example, if they have an important presentation tomorrow, ask them to come up with solutions for the problem on paper. Some examples of problems, in this case, may include:

- Missing the school bus
- Forgetting an important, presentation-related accessory
- Getting stage fright
- Forgetting your rehearsed lines

Give them five minutes to think of possible solutions—as many as they can think of—to counter the situation they are in. Whoever comes up with the most practical and workable solution wins.

Scavenger Hunt

Scavenger hunts are a classic and fun game for the whole family. They can make for an interesting game night where the whole family takes part in it. You can divide all family members into two groups and have them search for something. You can even add your own twist to it by making it a to-do scavenger hunt. Here, each team will be presented with a list of activities—some in the forms of plain clues, riddles, jokes to decipher, etc.—that they must complete to win points. Each game can have a different theme or task. An example of activities can include the following:

- Drink a glass of milk to find the clue to find your first clue under the bottle in the fridge
- Skip a rope 10 times before moving forward
- Finish the lyrics to a Christmas song for the next clue
- Bring something from the dresser that a parent uses often
- Solve a sudoku puzzle to get your next clue.

The team that finishes all the activities and collects all the points wins.

What Do You Think?

In this game, players ask each other open-ended questions to foster creative- and critical-thinking skills. Open-ended questions can't have right or wrong answers. It reveals how one views things. Since different people can have different perspectives, this can be an interesting game to get to know your child better. These questions can each be based on a hypothetical problem where the child has to come up with a solution. For example, you can ask them:

- What would you do in an exam if you forgot to pack your pencil box?

- What will you do if you get stuck in an elevator all alone?
- What will you do if you are home alone with no food?
- How will plants grow if the sun doesn't come out one day?
- What will you do if you get lost in a park without Mommy and Daddy?

Guess Who I Am?

In this game, the idea is to help children guess a famous celebrity or people close to them. All you need to do is think of someone famous your child knows about and research a few facts about them. These facts can be related to their personality, appearance, or work/field. The guesser can ask five questions before answering the person they think it is. Such games not only help children think harder and use their imagination, but they also help with the development of great problem-solving skills in them.

Chapter 7:

Nurture a Growth Mindset

As children, we remember spending hours learning new things. From drinking water from a glass for the first time to learning to walk, or from using the public restroom to making a friend on the first day of school, we learned something every day. However, as we grew older, the learning stopped. It no longer remained an important part of our lives. We succumbed to the pressures of the world and gave up with imagination and out-of-the-box thinking. We let the reality set in and take away our love for learning.

According to Carol Dweck (2006), our attitudes and beliefs shape our mindset. If we believe that we can't learn something new and resourceful, change our circumstances, or start over, we have a fixed mindset. On the other hand, some people believe that learning never stops, change is good and exciting, and starting over means more experience to back yourself on. These are the people with a growth mindset. Luckily, a mindset can be changed, altered, and molded. We can overcome our fears, accept change, and start afresh.

Victims of a fixed mindset would say otherwise. They believe that we are born with the skills and talents we have. Our traits are fixed. Some are naturally talented and gifted, and others aren't. They don't believe in learning something new or honing an existing skill for improvement. When they think there is no point in practicing, they give up. They dismiss all chances and opportunities that come their way, thinking it's not something they were made to succeed in.

An individual with a growth mindset views challenges and failures as learning opportunities. They view them as a golden ticket for growth. They aren't naturally smart, but they make sure that they gain more knowledge and expertise that would help them succeed in life. People with a growth mindset focus on progress—not the result. They look for prospects that will help them stretch their existing abilities. They believe they can improve their intelligence and personality with the right tools and thinking. They believe that nothing is carved in stone, and if they set their mind to something, they can learn it. You can often view them challenging themselves in the face of new problems and giving their best to overcome them.

This is the kind of mindset that we need to harness in our children, too. A growth mindset is an important ingredient for success and improved intelligence. With more knowledge, grit, and wisdom, children can thrive in a competitive world successfully. They can succeed in life when they choose to work hard and give their best effort.

It's All in the Head: A 10-Step Guide to Cultivating a Growth Mindset

Now that we understand the difference between the two mindsets and how they shape our thinking and skills, how we nurture them in our children seems like the next logical question. Although there are many strategies and steps to foster a growth mindset in children, here's a 10-step process to get you started.

1. *Focus On the Struggle*

Learning something new can be frustrating for children. They need a reason, a solid one, to be exact as to why they are doing something. They need to know how their contribution, focus, and efforts are going to help them and others. If they find that cause worthy, they will show interest. If not, they will make excuses and deliberately perform badly.

2. *Set Achievable Goals*

Every child learns at their own pace. Therefore, goals should be clear, relatable, and most importantly, achievable. A growth mindset won't develop if children feel the expectations are too high or too low. Make goals appropriate.

3. *Model Persistence*

Persistence teaches us that despite setbacks, we must continue on our journey forward. Modeling good persistence skills can help children stay positive and confident. They can overcome adversities with a positive and patient mind.

4. *Be Excited About Challenges*

When children enjoy challenges, they don't give up easily. The more conditioned they become, the more effort they put in.

5. *Encourage Risk-Taking*

Change is scary. It can make children take a step back instead of forward. However, if you push them a little and assure them that it is safe, they may try. If the goal is developmentally appropriate for their age, encourage them to go for it—even if it means going out of their comfort zone a bit.

6. *Embrace Imperfection*

No one is perfect. We all have different strengths and weaknesses: That is the beauty of it. Embracing who they are and not shying away from their weaknesses also helps with the cultivation of a growth mindset.

7. Don't Seek Validation

When we stop doing things to please others or appear superior to others, we rarely do things out of raw interest. We simply do them for fame and appreciation. However, the minute you stop seeking approval and focus on learning, that's when you start to grow. Let your child know that!

8. Value the Journey—Not the End

Intelligent people value learning more than the result. Even when they fail, they don't feel like a failure. They are all about sportsmanship. That is how they continue to grow and succeed.

9. Reward Action

Traits and talents aren't worth the reward, but action is. Every step taken in the right direction is worth a reward—no matter what the result. As parents, be sure to appreciate effort and action—even small wins.

10. Create a Sense of Purpose

Cultivating a sense of purpose bigger than themselves is also important. Always keep in mind the big picture so that the child remains motivated and eager for success.

Activities That Promote Positivity and Hope

There are many ways to change a fixed mindset. You start with instilling hope of a better future in their minds. Then, you provide them with the right resources, including your guidance and support. During the course of learning/trying something new, you keep reminding them how well they are doing and how proud you are. If they encounter a roadblock, you instill resilience and perseverance in them.

As they begin to see that anything is possible, you raise your expectation but also provide the means and knowledge they would need.

There are many creative ways to do so. Below are five to help you get started.

Prepare Affirmations

Positive affirmations are an excellent way to keep looking at the bright side of things and staying positive. The right growth affirmations can change the way children approach new challenges. They can foster positivity and hope. Create a list of affirmations together and write them on a chart. Place that where it's most visible. Tell your child to repeat those affirmations to themselves every day with confidence and certainty.

Some examples of phrases and sentences can look like this:

- I am the best version of myself.
- I think, I create, and I succeed.
- I can do hard things.
- Challenges excite me.
- Failure makes me stronger.

Use the Power of Yet

The power of yet is an excellent activity and practice. To incorporate the power of yet in your child's life requires that you ask them to list some things they can't do. Once they have the list, ask them to add the word "yet" at the end of each sentence. Show them how powerful adding a simple three-letter word at the end of the sentence induces hope and positivity. Encourage them to apply the same philosophy with everything they think they can't do. This tells them that learning is a never-ending process, and it is the journey that matters. Some examples of sentences include:

- I can't ride a bike… yet.
- I can't sleep with the light off… yet.
- I can't present my poem in front of everyone at school… yet.

Try 30-Day Challenges

Any 30-day challenges are a great way to bring a shift in the mindset from negative to positive. Learning never stops. However, trying to replace old habits with new ones can be difficult. Therefore, to ease the transition, take one step every day. Divide a big goal into smaller goals and try to accomplish one every day. The idea is to reach the end goal without any stops or pauses in between. That is how habits become natural.

You and your child can decide on a goal together and then divide it into smaller challenges expanded over a month. Some fun ideas for 30-day growth mindset challenges can look something like this:

- Stop wasting time
- Read something new every day
- Trying something new every day
- Learning to do chores

Research Famous Failures

On days when your child feels hopeless and discouraged, research a list of celebrities, scientists, writers, and athletes who continued with grit despite the many failures and struggles they faced. Tell them how J.K. Rowling's *Harry Potter* manuscript was rejected by 12 major publications. Remind them that their beloved host, Oprah Winfrey, was told by producers that she was too ugly to be on TV. If they love cartoons, tell them that the creator Walt Disney was fired from his job because the editors told him he lacked imagination.

Reading about the failures and struggles of others can also help foster a positive mindset. Children can see that it isn't the end of the world and that their struggles are too trivial compared to the ones you talk to them about.

Question Yourself

Another intelligent and creative way to make children rethink their struggles, choices, and decisions is to ask them questions related to their day, school, and homework. For example, you can ask them the following:

- What did you accomplish today that looked hard?
- What skills would you like to get better at?
- What new knowledge did you gain today?
- What is that one thing you have gotten better at recently?
- What is the one thing you would like to accomplish by the end of the month?

Chapter 8:

Become a Gardener

Every child is unique and precious. They all have different proclivities and interests. As parents, we must nurture their uniqueness and creativity. Given the competitiveness of today, many parents feel like they have to spoon-feed their children everything. They believe that they have to raise children that get into their desired colleges easily, pay off student loans with prospering jobs, and find someone to love and share their life with.

It's true that you might want that, too. However, your job is to nurture goodness and intelligence in them—not hover over every detail of their lives. You don't have to enroll them in courses they aren't interested in but promise success. At the end of the day, we need to relax and step back.

Our children will shine on their own using their light. They will grow into amazing, kind, and smart adults, provided that we offer them our attention, love, and care.

This requires that we build a gardener's mindset instead of a carpenter's mindset.

In this final chapter of the book, there are no steps or activities but rather advice from one parent to another.

As Alison Gopnik discusses in her book, *The Gardener and the Carpenter* (Gopnik, 2017), we need to give up trying to control every detail of our children's lives. We need to let them decide who they want to be, what they want to do, and what they think is the best thing for them. We need to stop with the manipulation, hovering, and pressure. What this does is only create needless anxiety in our children about their futures. Instead of exploring and harnessing their abilities, they become afraid. What if society rejects them? What if everyone laughs in their face? What if they fail to live up to everyone's expectations?

They stop taking risks or being remotely creative.

A carpenter parent is a hands-on parenting style. It involves a lot of instructions and rules. Like a carpenter that builds a house, a parent believes that their actions should be measured, cut, and calculated. They want to shape the child into an ideal they imagined without asking what the child wants. They think a child can be molded if they receive the right skills, read the right books, and do the right things. However, this isn't always true. No evidence suggests this. Sure, it may improve their existing skills and make them more admirable, but it doesn't guarantee success because the child had little to do with it.

A gardener, on the other hand, is a more hands-off parenting style. Here, parents don't force a child to grow into the desired ideal. They simply attend to their core needs and let the child explore and imagine. It's like they provide nutrient-rich soil to the plant, unfurl its leaves, place it in the sun, and let the flowers bloom. The idea is to provide children with a nourishing environment and become what they are meant to become.

There is little control and manipulation. The child grows at their own pace in a protected and loved environment. The environment is rich, nourishing, variable, and diverse.

So what parents should do is try to cultivate a gardener. Let them lead with full autonomy, solve their problems, and explore new worlds.

Only then can they be intelligent, creative, resilient, and happy.

Conclusion

Raising wise, sensible, and intelligent children is the dream of every parent. They believe that more knowledge and expertise are what results in success. However, the secret isn't that straightforward. Intelligence relies not only on how much one knows but rather a collection of skills, talents, and amount of time children spend doing something productive.

In this book, we looked at how parents can raise wise and smart adults using seven principles. Since social skills building is an important predictor of intelligence and academic success, we looked at how parents can use various activities, games, and practices to build healthy social skills in children. We also learned of the importance of reading and its long-term impact on a child's mind. As studies suggest, it opens new gateways of knowledge about the world, people, and cultures.

In the fourth chapter, we talked about how reducing screen time is beneficial. Various studies confirmed that too much screen time lowered a child's IQ. Therefore, we talked about games and activities that stimulated the brain instead and trained it to be more attentive, focused, and vigilant.

In the following chapters, we looked at the need for raising a problem solver with a growth mindset. We looked at how changing one's mindset and dealing with problems with grit and resilience is the way to boost intelligence.

The last secret looked at garnering a gardener's attitude in parents. It talked about how parents should give children the autonomy to be themselves while ensuring a healthy environment at home.

Hopefully, this book will guide new and experienced parents wishing to raise independent, happy, and smart children using practical strategies and activities.

Lastly, remember that your trust in their abilities is the greatest gift they can have. Learn to love them and spend time together by exploring new things. Exposure to new things and happy memories of the time you spend together is what shall make them successful.

Thank you for giving this book a read. I hope you loved reading it as much as I enjoyed writing it. It would make me the happiest person on earth if you would take a moment to leave an honest review. All you have to do is visit the site where you purchased this book: It's that simple! The review doesn't have to be a full-fledged paragraph; a few words will do. Your few words will help others decide if this is what they should be reading as well. Thank you in advance, and best of luck with your parenting adventures. Every moment is a joyous one with a child.

References

Arora, M. (2018, September 26). *15 exciting and fun reading games & activities for kids*. Parenting.firstcry.com. https://parenting.firstcry.com/articles/15-interesting-reading-games-and-activities-for-children/

Becker-Weidman, E. G., Jacobs, R. H., Reinecke, M. A., Silva, S. G., & March, J. S. (2010). Social problem-solving among adolescents treated for depression. *Behaviour Research and Therapy*, *48*(1), 11–18. https://doi.org/10.1016/j.brat.2009.08.006

Berns, G. S., Blaine, K., Prietula, M. J., & Pye, B. E. (2013). Short- and long-term effects of a novel on connectivity in the brain. *Brain Connectivity*, *3*(6), 590–600. https://doi.org/10.1089/brain.2013.0166

Borner, K. B., Gayes, L. A., & Hall, J. A. (2015). Friendship during childhood and cultural variations. *International Encyclopedia of the Social & Behavioral Sciences*, 442–447. https://doi.org/10.1016/b978-0-08-097086-8.23184-x

Briggs, S. (2017, March 2). *25 ways to develop A growth mindset in children*. TeachThought. https://www.teachthought.com/learning/develop-growth-mindset/

Buchweitz, A., Mason, R. A., Tomitch, L. M. B., & Just, M. A. (2009). Brain activation for reading and listening comprehension: An fMRI study of modality effects and individual differences in language comprehension. *Psychology & Neuroscience*, *2*(2), 111–123. https://doi.org/10.3922/j.psns.2009.2.003

Can reading improve your intelligence? Scientists say yes. (n.d.). Florida Prepaid College Board. Retrieved January 25, 2022, from https://www.myfloridaprepaid.com/collegedefinitely/can-reading-improve-intelligence-scientists-say-yes/#:~:text=They%20found%20that%20differences%20in

Cattell, R. B. (1963). Theory of fluid and crystallized intelligence: A critical experiment. *Journal of Educational Psychology*, *54*(1), 1–22. https://doi.org/10.1037/h0046743

Cherry, K. (2015). *How you can strengthen your brain with exercises*. Verywell Mind. https://www.verywellmind.com/brain-exercises-to-strengthen-your-mind-2795039

Cherry, K. (2019, October 8). *How psychologists evaluate intelligence.* Verywell Mind. https://www.verywellmind.com/theories-of-intelligence-2795035

Cherry, K. (2020, March 19). *Alfred Binet and the History of IQ Testing.* Verywell Mind. https://www.verywellmind.com/history-of-intelligence-testing-2795581

Developing problem solving skills in children. (2017, April). Kumon UK. https://www.kumon.co.uk/blog/developing-problem-solving-skills-in-children/

Durham, S. (2018, August 21). *The different types of intelligence: Which type are you?* SACAP. https://www.sacap.edu.za/blog/applied-psychology/types-of-intelligence/

Dweck, C. (2006). *Mindset: The New Psychology of Success.* Random House Publishing Group.

Elias, M. J., & Haynes, N. M. (2008). Social competence, social support, and academic achievement in minority, low-income, urban elementary school children. *School Psychology Quarterly*, *23*(4), 474–495. https://doi.org/10.1037/1045-3830.23.4.474

Fancourt, D., & Steptoe, A. (2019). Television viewing and cognitive decline in older age: Findings from the english longitudinal study of ageing.

Scientific Reports, *9*(1). https://doi.org/10.1038/s41598-019-39354-4

Fields, D. (2015, May 4). *Watching TV alters children's brain structure and lowers IQ*. Www.brainfacts.org. https://www.brainfacts.org/thinking-sensing-and-behaving/childhood-and-adolescence/2015/watching-tv-alters-childrens-brain-structure-and-lowers-iq#:~:text=Tests%20confirmed%20that%20the%20children

Gao, Q., Chen, W., Wang, Z., & Lin, D. (2019). Secret of the masters: Young chess players show advanced visual perspective taking. *Frontiers in Psychology*, *10*. https://doi.org/10.3389/fpsyg.2019.02407

Gardner, H. (1983). *Frames of Mind: The Theory of Multiple Intelligences*. Basic Books.

Global Council on Brain Health. (2017). *Engage your brain: GCBH recommendations on cognitively stimulating activities*. https://www.aarp.org/content/dam/aarp/health/brain_health/2017/07/gcbh-cognitively-stimulating-activities-report-english-aarp.doi.10.26419%252Fpia.00001.001.pdf

Gopnik, A. (2017). *The gardener and the carpenter : What the new science of child development tells us about the relationship between parents and children*. St Martins Pr.

Gutierrez, E. (2012, May 11). *Problem-solving skills are an important factor in academic success.* MSU Extension. https://www.canr.msu.edu/news/problem_solving_skills_are_an_important_factor_in_academic_success

Hochwarter, W. A., Witt, L. A., Treadway, D. C., & Ferris, G. R. (2006). The interaction of social skill and organizational support on job performance. *Journal of Applied Psychology*, *91*(2), 482–489. https://doi.org/10.1037/0021-9010.91.2.482

How to help children develop a growth mindset. (n.d.). Kaplan. Retrieved January 26, 2022, from https://www.kaplanco.com/ii/help-children-develop-a-growth-mindset

How to measure intelligence? (6 ways) | psychology. (2018, April 24). Psychology Discussion - Discuss Anything about Psychology. https://www.psychologydiscussion.net/intelligence/how-to-measure-intelligence-6-ways-psychology/13608

Importance of problem solving skills in your child |. (2020, February 22). Early Childhood University. https://theearlychildhooduniversity.com/importance-of-problem-solving-skills-and-how-to-nurture-them-in-your-child/

Indeed Editorial Team. (2019). *Social skills: Definition and examples.* Indeed.com.

https://www.indeed.com/career-advice/career-development/social-skills

Ingber, S. (2018, May 28). What kind of parent are you: Carpenter or gardener? *NPR.org*. https://www.npr.org/sections/goatsandsoda/2018/05/28/614386847/what-kind-of-parent-are-you-carpenter-or-gardener#:~:text=The%20%22carpenter%22%20thinks%20that%20his

Intelligence and Creativity. (n.d.). OER Services. https://courses.lumenlearning.com/suny-fmcc-intropsych/chapter/what-are-intelligence-and-creativity/

Jenn. (2021, March 14). *17 easy growth mindset activities for kids (& adults).* Healthy Happy Impactful. https://healthyhappyimpactful.com/growth-mindset-activities-kids-adults/

Jerrim, J., Lopez-Agudo, L. A., & Marcenaro-Gutierrez, O. D. (2020). Does it matter what children read? New evidence using longitudinal census data from spain. *Oxford Review of Education*, *46*(5), 515–533. https://doi.org/10.1080/03054985.2020.1723516

Katz, L. & Rubin, M. (1998). *Keep Your Brain Alive: 83 Neurobic Exercises to Help Prevent Memory Loss and Increase Mental Fitness.* Workman Publishing Company.

Kidd, D. C., & Castano, E. (2013). Reading literary fiction improves theory of mind. *Science, 342*(6156), 377–380. https://doi.org/10.1126/science.1239918

Kohnle, D. (2013, August 27). *Health tip: Kids shouldn't watch too much TV*. MedicineNet; MedicineNet. https://www.medicinenet.com/script/main/art.asp?articlekey=173048

Krell-Roesch, J., Vemuri, P., Pink, A., Roberts, R. O., Stokin, G. B., Mielke, M. M., Christianson, T. J. H., Knopman, D. S., Petersen, R. C., Kremers, W. K., & Geda, Y. E. (2017). Association between mentally stimulating activities in late life and the outcome of incident mild cognitive impairment, with an analysis of the APOE ε4 genotype. *JAMA Neurology*, *74*(3), 332. https://doi.org/10.1001/jamaneurol.2016.3822

Kyllonen, P. C., & Christal, R. E. (1990). Reasoning ability is (little more than) working-memory capacity?! *Intelligence*, *14*(4), 389–433. https://doi.org/10.1016/s0160-2896(05)80012-1

Mae, K. (2019, January 11). *Why being A "carpenter parent" can be harmful to kids.* Scary Mommy. https://www.scarymommy.com/parenting-style-carpenter-versus-gardener/

Mann, S. B. (2019, April 12). *17 fun problem solving activities & games [for kids, adults and teens].*

Icebreaker Ideas. https://icebreakerideas.com/problem-solving-activities/

Marchal, J. (2016, May 13). *How to raise smart kids: Unmissable secrets of parenting.* Lifehack. https://www.lifehack.org/400864/how-to-raise-smart-kids-unmissable-secrets-of-parenting

Mastroianni, B. (2019, March 10). *Binge-Watching TV can dull your brain.* Healthline. https://www.healthline.com/health-news/binge-watching-tv-can-dull-your-brain

Measures of intelligence. (n.d.). OER Services. https://courses.lumenlearning.com/wsu-sandbox/chapter/measures-of-intelligence/

Measuring intelligence | boundless psychology. (2013). OER Services. https://courses.lumenlearning.com/boundless-psychology/chapter/measuring-intelligence/

Mehta, K. (2021, March 10). *A harvard psychologist says humans have 8 types of intelligence. which ones do you score the highest in?* CNBC. https://www.cnbc.com/2021/03/10/harvard-psychologist-types-of-intelligence-where-do-you-score-highest-in.html

Morin, A. (2019). *Teach kids how to solve their own problems and make good decisions.* Verywell Family.

https://www.verywellfamily.com/teach-kids-problem-solving-skills-1095015

Morin, A. (2020, May 18). *8 activities to encourage pre-reading and early literacy*. Verywell Family. https://www.verywellfamily.com/activities-to-encourage-pre-reading-621060

Morin, A. (2021, February 27). *7 social skills you should start teaching your child now*. Verywell Family. https://www.verywellfamily.com/seven-social-skills-for-kids-4589865#toc-benefits

Naglieri, J. A. (2020, May 13). *Thinking versus knowing: The key to measuring intelligence*. National Association of School Psychologists (NASP). https://www.nasponline.org/professional-development/a-closer-look/thinking-versus-knowing-the-key-to-measuring-intelligence

Panfiloff, E. (n.d.). *Does reading books increase your IQ?* EnhancingBrain.com. https://enhancingbrain.com/does-reading-books-increase-your-iq/

Park, D. C., Lodi-Smith, J., Drew, L., Haber, S., Hebrank, A., Bischof, G. N., & Aamodt, W. (2013). The impact of sustained engagement on cognitive function in older adults. *Psychological Science*, *25*(1), 103–112. https://doi.org/10.1177/0956797613499592

Peck, S. (2019, February 12). *Why a growth mindset is essential for learning - learn to code in 30 days.* Learn to Code in 30 Days. https://learn.onemonth.com/why-a-growth-mindset-is-essential-for-learning/

Pillai, J. A., Hall, C. B., Dickson, D. W., Buschke, H., Lipton, R. B., & Verghese, J. (2011). Association of crossword puzzle participation with memory decline in persons who develop dementia. *Journal of the International Neuropsychological Society : JINS*, *17*(6). https://doi.org/10.1017/S1355617711001111

Positive Action Staff. (2020, October 14). 20 evidence-based social skills activities and games for kids. *Positive Action.* https://www.positiveaction.net/blog/social-skills-activities-and-games-for-kids

Ravi, A. (2021, May 13). *15 fun activities to teach problem solving to kids.* MomJunction. https://www.momjunction.com/articles/how-to-teach-problem-solving-for-kids-activities_00733680/

Ritchie, S. J., Bates, T. C., & Plomin, R. (2014). Does learning to read improve intelligence? A longitudinal multivariate analysis in identical twins from age 7 to 16. *Child Development*, *86*(1), 23–36. https://doi.org/10.1111/cdev.12272

Rosiek, A., Maciejewska, N., Leksowski, K., Rosiek-Kryszewska, A., & Leksowski, Ł. (2015). Effect of television on obesity and excess of weight and consequences of health. *International Journal of Environmental Research and Public Health*, *12*(8), 9408–9426. https://doi.org/10.3390/ijerph120809408

Spearman, C. (1904). "General intelligence," objectively determined and measured. *The American Journal of Psychology*, *15*(2), 201–293. https://doi.org/10.2307/1412107

Stangor, C., & Walinga, J. (2019). Introduction to psychology. In *openpress.usask.ca*. BCcampus. https://opentextbc.ca/introductiontopsychology/

Suk, N. (2017). The effects of extensive reading on reading comprehension, reading rate, and vocabulary acquisition. *Reading Research Quarterly*, *52*(1), 73–89. https://www.jstor.org/stable/26622579

Szwed, M., Ventura, P., Querido, L., Cohen, L., & Dehaene, S. (2011). Reading acquisition enhances an early visual process of contour integration. *Developmental Science*, *15*(1), 139–149. https://doi.org/10.1111/j.1467-7687.2011.01102.x

Takeuchi, H., Taki, Y., Hashizume, H., Asano, K., Asano, M., Sassa, Y., Yokota, S., Kotozaki, Y.,

Nouchi, R., & Kawashima, R. (2013). The impact of television viewing on brain structures: Cross-Sectional and longitudinal analyses. *Cerebral Cortex*, *25*(5), 1188–1197. https://doi.org/10.1093/cercor/bht315

The eight types of intelligence. (n.d.). Iberostar. https://www.iberostar.com/en/inspiration-guide/wellness/eight-types-of-intelligence/

Thurstone, L. L. (1973). Primary mental abilities. *The Measurement of Intelligence*, 131–136. https://doi.org/10.1007/978-94-011-6129-9_8

Twardowski, K. (2018, February 27). *Does reading make you smarter? Books and the brain.* Book Riot. https://bookriot.com/does-reading-make-you-smarter/

Warneken, F., Lohse, K., Melis, A. P., & Tomasello, M. (2010). Young children share the spoils after collaboration. *Psychological Science*, *22*(2), 267–273. https://doi.org/10.1177/0956797610395392

Why is problem solving important in child development? (2020, March 19). Www.marlborough.org. https://www.marlborough.org/news/~board/health-and-wellness/post/why-is-problem-solving-important-in-child-development#:~:text=Typically%2C%20effective%20problem%2Dsolving%20skills

Wise, A. (2015, January 8). *8 science-backed reasons to read a (real) book*. Real Simple; Real Simple. https://www.realsimple.com/health/preventative-health/benefits-of-reading-real-books

www.ingramcontent.com/pod-product-compliance
Lightning Source LLC
LaVergne TN
LVHW051016080826
845145LV00009B/2648

* 9 7 8 1 9 5 6 0 1 8 2 9 5 *